BOYZONE
CAUGHT ON CAMERA
BY TOP OF THE POPS

By Jeremy Mark & Simeon Jewkes

BBC

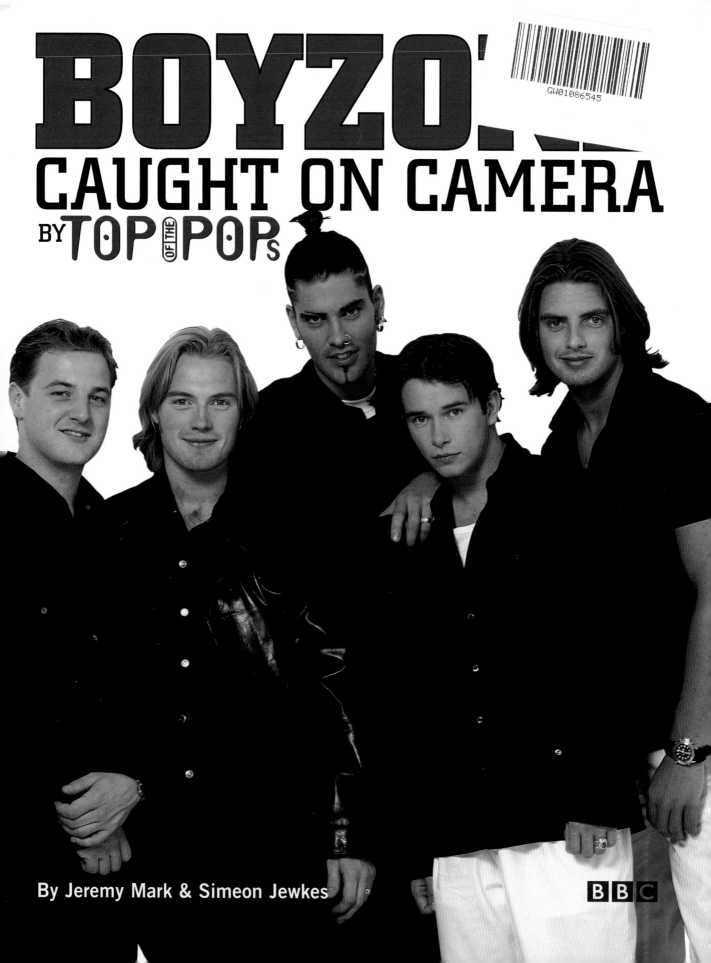

Top Of The Pops Boyzone Caught On Camera
First published in 1998 by BBC Worldwide Ltd
Woodlands, 80 Wood Lane, London W12 OTT

Based on material from *Top Of The Pops Magazine* and
Live & Kicking Magazine.

ISBN 0 563 38091 8

Colour Origination by Kestrel Digital Colour.

Printed by Jarrold Book Printing.

RONAN
KEITH
MIKEY
SHANE
STEPHEN
BOYZONE
CAUGHT ON CAMERA

R

Ronan

I'D LIKE TO FIND SOMEONE AND SETTLE DOWN. I KNOW I'M YOUNG, BUT I'M LONELY. IT'S HARD BEING ON THE ROAD AND I WANT SOMEONE I CAN COME BACK HOME TO.

— RONAN

I DON'T SEE MYSELF AS A SEX-SYMBOL. I JUST GET UP IN THE MORNING AND ACT THE WAY I'VE ALWAYS ACTED. I LOOK AFTER MYSELF — I LIKE TO WEAR NICE CLOTHES AND LOOK GOOD — BUT I DON'T STAND IN FRONT OF THE MIRROR GOING, 'COR, YOU'RE NICE!' THAT'S NOT MY THING.

— RONAN

THE LITTLE
devil !!

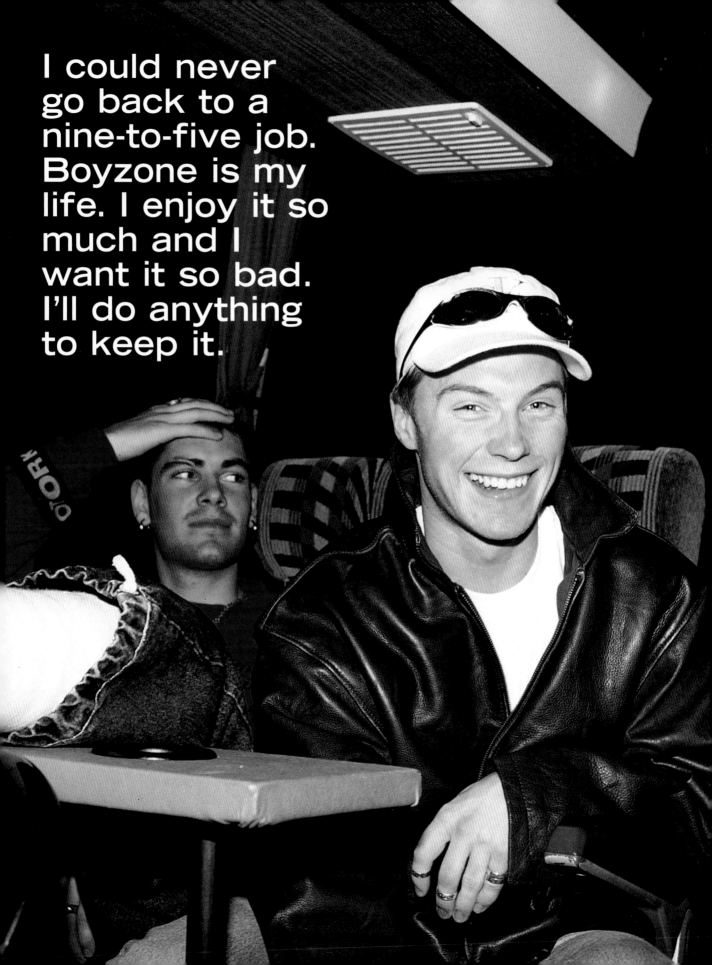

I could never go back to a nine-to-five job. Boyzone is my life. I enjoy it so much and I want it so bad. I'll do anything to keep it.

I'm not really one for chatting up girls, I don't know how to — honest. I'm not very good at that at all. I'm a shy kinda guy.
— Ronan

I REALLY LOVED BEING IN THE CHOIR AT PRIMARY SCHOOL, BUT I WAS ASKED TO LEAVE. WELL, NO, I WASN'T ACTUALLY ASKED, THE TEACHER JUST DIDN'T INVITE ME BACK, SO I GOT THE HINT AFTER A WHILE. I SHOULD GO BACK AND SEE HER NOW, SHOULDN'T I?!

— RONAN

I ALWAYS HAD THE FEELING THAT I'D MAKE SOMETHING OF MYSELF BECAUSE I HAD THE CONFIDENCE TO FOLLOW MY DREAMS.

HAS SUCCESS CHANGED ME? I HAVEN'T GOT BIG-HEADED OR ANYTHING, BUT I'VE DEFINITELY CHANGED. WE'VE ALL HAD A TASTE OF A BETTER LIFE AND WE LIKE IT. IT'S NOT A BAD THING AS LONG AS YOU DON'T START TAKING ANYTHING FOR GRANTED. I'VE GONE OVER AND OVER IT IN MY HEAD AND AS LONG AS YOU KNOW WHAT YOU'RE ABOUT AND REMEMBER WHERE YOU'VE COME FROM, THAT'S THE IMPORTANT THING.

— RONAN

WHAT SCARES ME THE MOST
IS THE THOUGHT OF NOT
BEING ABLE TO PLEASE OUR
FANS ANY MORE. THERE'S
ALWAYS A HEART-STOPPING
MOMENT WHEN WE RELEASE
A NEW SINGLE, WONDERING
WHERE IT WILL GO IN THE
CHARTS. WE'RE OFTEN ASKED
HOW WE FEEL ABOUT THE
SUCCESS OF NEWER BANDS,
BUT IT'S NOT A COMPETITION.
WE'LL JUST DO WHATEVER IT
TAKES TO KEEP MAKING OUR
FANS HAPPY.   — RONAN

Keith

I WON'T SETTLE DOWN FOR A GOOD WHILE YET. I'VE GOT A BABY AND A GIRLFRIEND, BUT I CAN'T STAY AT HOME FOR TOO LONG. I'VE GOT ANTS IN MY PANTS, I HAVE TO BE ON THE ROAD, I LOVE BEING OUT PARTYING. IF BOYZONE EVER ENDS I'LL GO STRAIGHT INTO SOMETHING ELSE. I CAN'T STAND THE THOUGHT OF A QUIET LIFE. – KEITH

I don't think **Keith** will ever change. He'll always be up for a major night out and I reckon in years to come, when he has grandkids, Keith will still be the wildest man in town. — **MIKEY**

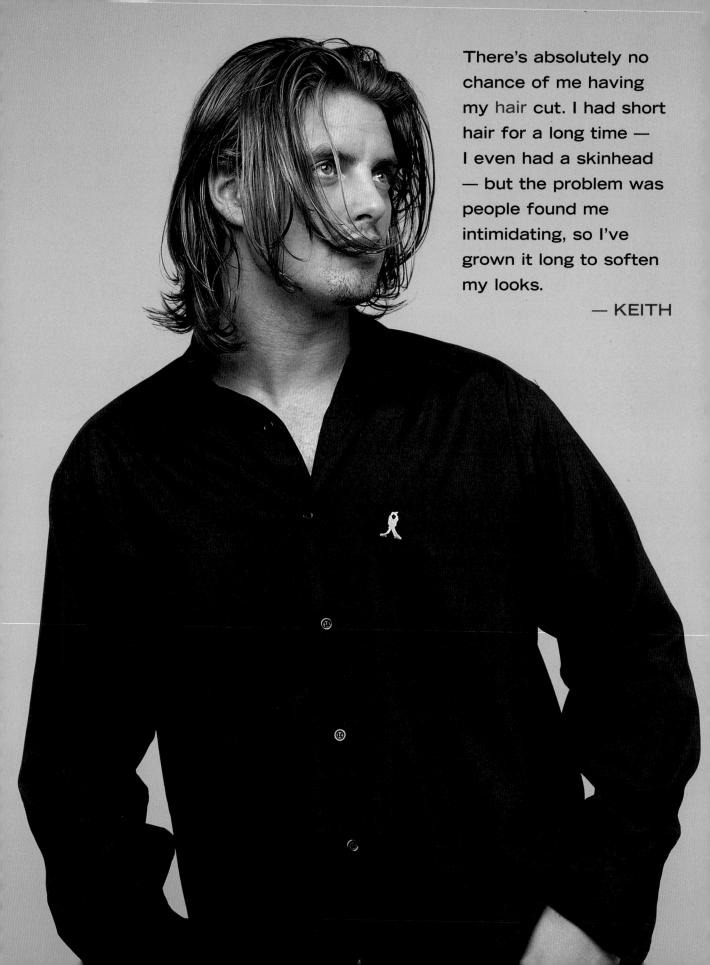

There's absolutely no chance of me having my hair cut. I had short hair for a long time — I even had a skinhead — but the problem was people found me intimidating, so I've grown it long to soften my looks.

— KEITH

EVERYONE THINKS I'M THE TOUGHEST IN THE BAND, BUT I'M JUST A BIG SOFTIE.   — KEITH

Mikey

I SELDOM REMEMBER MY DREAMS, BUT ONCE OR TWICE I REMEMBER DREAMING ABOUT ONE PARTICULAR GIRL. I DON'T KNOW WHO SHE WAS, BUT I WOKE UP IN THE MORNING COMPLETELY IN LOVE WITH HER. — MIKEY

I must confess that I'm not at all confident about the way I look. I especially feel it when there are thousands of girls screaming at us. When you're under the spotlight, you constantly feel you're being scrutinised.

— MIKEY

IF I WAS TO RETIRE
TOMORROW, I'D
DEFINITELY BE HAPPY.
OVER THE LAST FIVE
YEARS, I'VE HAD A
GREAT TIME AND
MADE FOUR REALLY
GOOD FRIENDS, WHICH
IS SOMETHING MONEY
CAN'T BUY.

— MIKEY

ON THE HEAD, SON!

Mikey will do anything for a laugh — and he's great at laughing at himself too.
— STEPHEN

Shane

THE BRILLIANT THING ABOUT SHANE IS THAT HE'S ALWAYS HAD THIS NATURAL COOLNESS ABOUT HIM. HE'S ALWAYS WANTED TO BE UNIQUE AND BOYZONE'S GIVEN HIM THE CHANCE TO BE THE PERSON HE'S ALWAYS WANTED TO BE. HE'S TOTALLY COME OUT OF HIS SHELL. – KEITH

PEOPLE OFTEN SAY THAT WHEN THEY FIRST MEET ME THEY IMMEDIATELY THINK I'M HARD, SERIOUS AND MAYBE A BIT IGNORANT. IN FACT, I'M THE COMPLETE OPPOSITE. I THINK IT'S BECAUSE I'M SO SHY AND QUIET THAT I TRY TO LOOK TOUGH. IT'S MY WAY OF BEING LOUD WITHOUT HAVING TO SHOUT ABOUT IT. IT'S MY WAY OF BEING NOTICED. I'M AN EXTREMIST. WHEN I DO SOMETHING, I DO IT TO THE FULL. – SHANE

I'm actually not very romantic at all. I can't actually think of one traditionally romantic thing I've ever done for a girl.
— SHANE

I'M VERY HAPPY. I NEVER DREAMED I'D GET THIS FAR. WHEN I WAS 12, MY SISTER BOUGHT A NEW KIDS ON THE BLOCK TAPE AND I GOT REALLY INTO IT. I REMEMBER THINKING, 'I'D LIKE TO DO THAT'. BUT BY 13, I'D FORGOTTEN ALL ABOUT IT — AND NOW LOOK AT ME!
— SHANE

Stephen

I don't cry as much as I used to. I used to cry quite a lot, but not in front of other people if I could help it. I'm trying to toughen myself up. You know, put up a barrier and be a little less sensitive.
— Stephen

I'VE WANTED TO SING A SONG FOR A DISNEY MOVIE FOR AS LONG AS I CAN REMEMBER. I COULDN'T BELIEVE IT WHEN THEY CALLED TO ASK IF I'D LIKE TO RECORD SHOOTING STAR FOR HERCULES AND OF COURSE I JUMPED AT THE CHANCE! WHENEVER I LISTEN TO THE SONG, I THINK TO MYSELF, 'I'VE BEEN VERY, VERY, VERY LUCKY.' AND ANYBODY OUT THERE WHO HAS DREAMS SHOULD DEFINITELY FOLLOW THEM, BECAUSE DREAMS REALLY CAN COME TRUE. MINE HAVE.

— STEPHEN

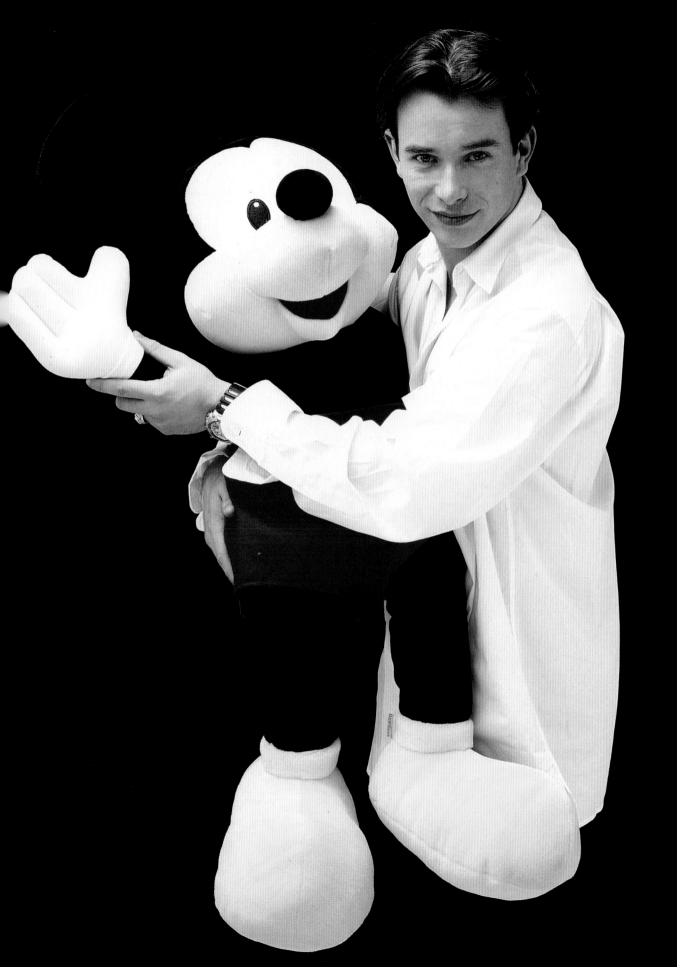

I'M NOT A REAL PARTY PERSON. I PREFER TO CHILL OUT, YOU KNOW RELAX AND READ A BOOK OR GO TO THE CINEMA. AT THE END OF THE DAY I'M USUALLY SO TIRED THAT I JUST FALL INTO MY BED. I DON'T THINK THERE'S MUCH CHANCE OF ME BURNING OUT SOMEHOW. — STEPHEN

Some people may think I lay myself open to being taken advantage of because I'm not hard enough, but I don't let that happen. I'm very, very sharp and can tell what people want from me, who's genuine and who's not. It's intuition.
— Stephen

I HAVE EXPERIENCED LOVE AT FIRST SIGHT. IT DIDN'T LAST, BUT IT HIT ME STRAIGHT AWAY, LIKE, 'WHAM!' AND IT FELT SO MUCH MORE SPECIAL THAN ANYTHING ELSE BEFORE. — STEPHEN

I don't think success will ever go to my head. I've learnt a lot and matured a lot, but I'll never forget where I've come from and that I didn't have a lot four years ago. I'm very proud of myself and the band, but I won't ever get big-headed or blow things out of proportion.

—Stephen

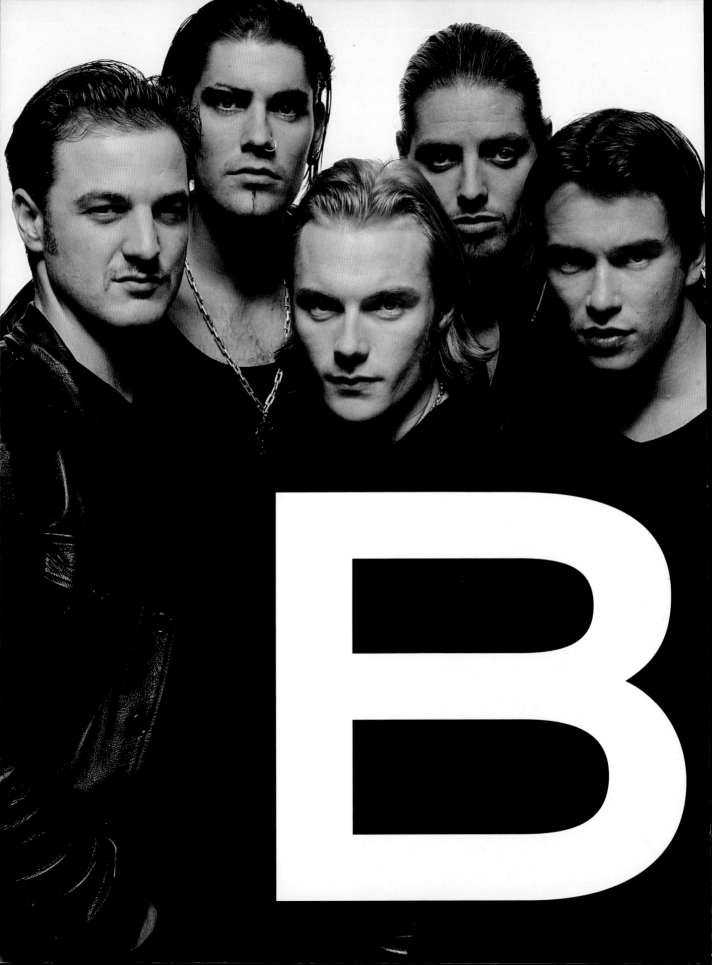

DON'T MISS

THANKS TO THE TOP OF THE POPs PHOTOGRAPHERS

David Boughton

Ray Burmiston

Neil Cooper

Jamie Fry

John Green

Robin Green

David Willis